ALL AB

8 WAYS TO REVERSE PCOS NATURALLY

DR. MONIKA BIJAKA AGRAWAL

Copyright © Dr. Monika Bijaka Agrawal
All Rights Reserved.

This book has been self-published with all reasonable efforts taken to make the material error-free by the author. No part of this book shall be used, reproduced in any manner whatsoever without written permission from the author, except in the case of brief quotations embodied in critical articles and reviews.

The Author of this book is solely responsible and liable for its content including but not limited to the views, representations, descriptions, statements, information, opinions and references ["Content"]. The Content of this book shall not constitute or be construed or deemed to reflect the opinion or expression of the Publisher or Editor. Neither the Publisher nor Editor endorse or approve the Content of this book or guarantee the reliability, accuracy or completeness of the Content published herein and do not make any representations or warranties of any kind, express or implied, including but not limited to the implied warranties of merchantability, fitness for a particular purpose. The Publisher and Editor shall not be liable whatsoever for any errors, omissions, whether such errors or omissions result from negligence, accident, or any other cause or claims for loss or damages of any kind, including without limitation, indirect or consequential loss or damage arising out of use, inability to use, or about the reliability, accuracy or sufficiency of the information contained in this book.

Made with ♥ on the Notion Press Platform
www.notionpress.com

"Om vakratunda mahakaya,

Suryakoti samaprabha,

Nirvighnam kurume deva ,

Sarv karyeshu sarvada !!

Om Ganganpataye namah:

"

Contents

Preface — vii

Foreword — ix

About The Author — xi

Acknowledgements — xiii

Prologue — xv

1. What Is Pcos? — 1
2. What Is Pcod? — 2
3. What Is The Main Difference Between Pcod And Pcos? — 3
4. Why: Pcod (polycystic Ovarian Syndrome) Happens? — 4
5. What Are The Symptoms Of Pcos ? — 6
6. How Can We Diagnose Pcos? — 7
7. Which Organs Are Included In The Pcos? — 8
8. When Can Pcos Happen In The Body? — 9
9. How Pcos Affects The Body In The Long Run ?: — 10
10. Is It Possible To Get Pregnant With Pcos ? — 11
11. Why It Is Important To Manage Weight & Glucose Levels In Pcos? — 12
12. What Type Of Food Can We Have In Pcos? — 13
13. What Kind Of Food Can We Take More Or Less In Our Diet? — 14
14. Is Fasting Helpful In Pcos? — 15
15. What Are The Natural Ways And Natural Easy Home Remedies For Pcos? — 16
16. What Changes In The Lifestyle Are Best For Pcod/pcos? — 18
17. How Does The Ayurveda Concept Help In Pcos? — 19

Contents

18. How Does Modern And Ancient Science Help In Pcos?	20
19. How Yoga Works On Pcos/pcod?	21
20. Which Yoga-asans Are Best During Pcos ?	23
21. How Can We Do Yoga In Less Than 15 Mins For Pcod/pcos?	54
22. How Can We Do Yoga For 30 Mins For Pcod/pcos?	56
23. How Can We Do Yoga For 60 Mins For Pcod/pcos?	58
24. How Does Naturopathy Work On Pcod/pcos?	61
25. Do's And Don'ts For Pcos?	62
26. Diet Pattern:	63
27. Can You Suggest A Suitable Food List For Pcos?	66
28. Do You Have Any Success Stories About Pcos?	68
Praise For Our Works	73
For Quick Refrences	77
Some Pictures About Yoga Health Care Centre	85
Social Media Presence	89

Preface

All About PCOS has all the basic information for every woman, from puberty to menopause, explaining all about menstruation, basic introduction of PCOS, symptoms, causes, effects in the body and also recommending some natural remedies with Yoga, food and lifestyle patterns. In this book, there are also naturopathic methods for better results. What are the aspects of ayurveda for PCOS and some easy home remedies are also given. Along with it, we have 3 different yoga modules for 15 minutes, 25 minutes and 60 minutes. As a bonus, we have provided a general food pattern that is easy to follow for people suffering with PCOS. We have also provided a food list about PCOS in order to clarify which foods to avoid, which food to have in plenty and which food to have in limited quantity. Some healthy food replacement options are also mentioned in the book. At the end, true and inspiring success story is also given to motivate others about using natural methods along with some reviews about the yoga, food and wellness methods.

Foreword

Every woman has three milestones or the most important three chapters of her life. First, it starts with menstruation, the second is pregnancy and delivery and the third one is Menopause. Thus, they are in the following order-
1) Menstruation
2) Pregnancy and delivery
3) Menopause.

So, here we will be talking about menstruation. This happens when a girl's body begins to change, and begins to grow into a woman. This stage of maturity starts from 9 years to 13 years. Also called, puberty, this is when physiological and hormonal changes take place in her body to help her start this beautiful journey of womanhood. During this time, hormones are at their peak to enable her to face the challenges that life throws with help of nature. This journey until the teenage girl turns into a woman helps to prepare her physically and mentally to become mother of a healthy baby. This period of growth during which a transition- from childhood to womanhood takes place, essential changes in your body and in your mind occurs, changes take place in ovaries, in the uterus, in your pituitary gland, in your body like increase of fat around your chest area and hips to protect your genital organs and internal organs. Entering womanhood, particularly, menstruation is a beautiful creation of Mother Nature, and is a period of change occurring in a female that happens each month. It is such a purely physiological process for preparing the female body for reproduction and biological functions. So a regular menstrual cycle is essential for proper functioning of the ovaries, the main female sex organs situated at the sides of the uterus which begin to function by producing an egg or ovum every month, leading to menstruation. This process starts between the age of 10-15 and remains till one turns 45-50 years of age. During this time, the lining of the uterus becomes soft and swollen to receive an ovum and produces excess blood to nourish it. When the ovum does not fertilize with the sperm and no zygote is formed, the blood is not needed for its nourishment and the swollen membranes of the uterus with excess blood is released from the uterus through the vagina in the form of blood discharge. This discharge takes place once a month. This is called menstruation and depends upon the hypothalamus which is closely connected with the pituitary gland. Yoga and Pranayam are of great help in this phase of life when the body undergoes changes to develop into a woman. This process makes sure to provide immense supply of nutrition to their weak organs and skeletal growth and to improve the shape of the body, so that this healthy lifestyle change is amongst the psychological changes and to make sure the right guidance is given at the right time. This also confirms that you have healthy menstruation in each stage of your life. Each mindset has its different aspect of self-consciousness in individuality asserting itself at this period in the woman's mind, as it becomes extra sensitive and the woman's behaviour seems like razor-sharp keen-nests so due to physiological and psychological changes in the body might make her stressed. So, yoga will surely help create a healthy atmosphere in proper guidance, which is a necessity during the menstruation period, during the puberty and the second milestone of every woman's life, pregnancy. If there is irregularity in one's menstruation cycles that is called PCOS (Polycystic Ovary Syndrome). In this book, we will discuss about PCOS in depth.

About The Author

Dr.Monika Bijaka Agrawal

Dr. Monika Bijaka Agrawal has been in this field since the year 2001. She has completed her Ph.D. in Yoga & Naturopathy. In academics, she received a Gold medal in Yoga & Naturopathy diploma in the year 2001. After that, she completed DNHE, CIG, and MA in yoga. Further, she completed a Cognitive fitness certificate course from Harvard Health Publishing along with multiple other certifications around health and wellness. She has presented research papers on treatment through yoga & naturopathy for menopausal problems, migraines, Obesity, Diet awareness & other women's health-related problems and has also written many articles in renowned yoga & naturopathy magazines.

She is the founder & director of Yoga Health Care Centre which is operational since 2001. The Centre was initially started in Jaipur and a branch was opened in Gurgaon in the year 2009. The center in Gurgaon is among the top 5 Yoga Centres in the city. In addition to the regular offline & online yoga classes (morning & evening), Pregnancy Yoga, Meditation sessions, and Shatkarma sessions and conducted, and Therapy, acupressure, Sujok, Diet consultation, and

ABOUT THE AUTHOR

Cupping therapy services are also provided.

She is passionate about Yoga & Naturopathy and She loves to manage disease aspects with this approach. She has also been elected as vice president of the International Naturopathy Organisation team in Gurgaon. She is now registered with Yoga Alliance US as ERYT200, RYT500, and YACEP, and our yoga school registered with this alliance as RYS200. Yoga Health Care Centre is also conducting Yoga Teacher Training courses for new students (RYT200) such as Basis & Advance Yoga Teacher Training Program, Pregnancy Yoga Teacher Training Program, Face Yoga Teacher Training Program, Medical Yoga Teacher Training Program, Ayurvedic Nutrition basic course, and many other important courses.

This book is also got **no.1 bestseller** in international bestseller (in 3 categories) on Amazon Kindle store

Connect on

www.yogahealthcarecentre.com
Insta handle @yogahealthcarecentre
YouTube handle @yogahealthcarecentre

Acknowledgements

Among all, I would like to thank and pay my tribute to the supreme soul, my lord Ganesha, and my parents who have always helped me pave the way of life ever since, my life partner, also my critic, support, and love, my dearest husband Sachin Agrawal, my daughter Kashvee who is 12 (little artist, published author, poetess @kashveescraft), my son a. k. a. my wonder boy Kaveesh who is 4 (enjoying his preschool journey), my brother and supporter Dr. Mohit Bijaka, all of my family and friends, and also all the students from Yoga Health Care Centre family from Jaipur and Gurgaon, who motivate me to explore new things to learn regarding yoga, food & naturopathy and wellness, all of my Teachers, well-wishers and all those who have supported me in every step of my yoga journey and my entire life. THANK YOU, EVERYONE...

Prologue

""JUST A PHASE OF LIFE it all started with fatigue, Brought me in great despair, my bones became fragile, And oily were my hair. My menstrual cycles were missing, my skin was now pale, my mood was now triggered and my hormones, about to fail. My days were unproductive, My work was often undone, My stomach was paining, My job was no longer fun. I gathered myself together, And dragged myself to the gynaecologist She diagnosed me And told me my ovaries had a cyst. I felt betrayed and stressed nothing seemed to work, not even the medicines or the disease that was supposed to lurk. I planned to keep strong, and research for some time. Little did I know, That Yoga was the way to shine? I regularly did Yoga, And ate all healthy food, Within 2 months of work, My life was again good I felt like I was alive, I felt much more active, My life was now more productive, And my body, more reactive. It's all thanks to Yoga and to the nature's way, for it has a cure, for every disease we suffer today. PCOS is just a phase a phase that will pass by with some help from Mother Nature, All you have to do is try...."*

created with love by @kashveescraft."

CHAPTER ONE

WHAT IS PCOS?

What is PCOS ?:

Polycystic Ovarian Syndrome is a group of symptoms for many problems that are said to be lifestyle disease. PCOS is hormonal imbalance in the body. Women with PCOS may experience two conditions:

1) Increased levels of androgens (such as testosterone, male hormone), which can have many effects on the body, including irregular menstrual cycles, increased hair growth, and acne.

2) Insulin resistance, which affects how your body uses glucose (sugar), the primary energy source for your body is decreased.

CHAPTER TWO

WHAT IS PCOD?

PCOD is a Lifestyle disease, a condition that affects the woman's ovaries, the reproductive organs that produce progesterone and estrogen hormones which help in regulating the cycle and also produce a small amount of hormone to control our periods. Around 20% of women in this world suffer from PCOS, as this has become a very common health issue nowadays that causes hormonal imbalance, which in turn results in irregular menstrual periods and, eventually, may lead to infertility and problems in pregnancy. This also triggers problems like diabetes, acne, and excessive & unwanted hair growth. PCOS is a metabolic disorder in which women are affected by hormonal imbalance in the reproductive years between the ages of 21 to 51 years due to increased levels of male hormones. The global prevalence of PCOS is estimated to be as high as 20%. The World Health Organization's (WHO) data suggests that approximately 116 million women are affected by PCOS globally.

CHAPTER THREE

WHAT IS THE MAIN DIFFERENCE BETWEEN PCOD AND PCOS?

What is the main difference between PCOD and PCOS?

In PCOD, the ovaries begin to release immature eggs, resulting in hormonal imbalances including swollen ovaries, among several other symptoms; in PCOS, endocrine disorders cause the ovaries to produce excess androgens, making eggs susceptible to cyst formation. So PCOS is a chronic version of PCOD. In starting days of the disease, one has mild symptoms and effects on the body, but in the long run, it affects the pancreas, body metabolism, and other organs too. This situation is called PCOS.

CHAPTER FOUR

WHY: PCOD (POLYCYSTIC OVARIAN SYNDROME) HAPPENS?

Why: PCOD (polycystic ovarian syndrome) happens?

Lifestyle can be called the main culprit, as it's scientifically proven that our lifestyle is becoming increasingly stressful. So, due to inactive lifestyle, our body becomes lethargic and our metabolic rate slows down and gets disturbed.

The following are reasons why PCOD happens-

1. High expectations of life also cause more stress and hustle, leading to many diseases

2. Easy food is processed and ready-to-cook food, high sugar intakes that has toxic chemicals, which are common amongst youngsters nowadays.

3. Lack of exercise.

4. Wrong food combinations.

5. Ruining the natural body clock system - late night work and usages of screens (TV, MOBILES, and LAPTOPS).

6. In adequate sleep

CHAPTER FIVE

WHAT ARE THE SYMPTOMS OF PCOS

What are the symptoms of PCOS ?

It's vital to understand that PCOS is a condition, which means that different women will undergo different symptoms. While some women may only have a very few symptoms, others could experience several like the below:

- 1. Irregular and delayed periods (less than 21 or more than 35 days are called irregular)
- 2. UNCONTROLLED Weight gain
- 3. Unwanted hair growth around the face, neck, and back
- 4. Pigmentation on the face and around the neck
- 5. Unusual hair fall- baldness, alopecia
- 6. Abnormal sugar metabolism
- 7. High cholesterol
- 8. Blood pressure irregularities
- 9. Anxiety symptoms
- 10. Depression and withdrawal symptoms for life
- 11. some weird food cravings

CHAPTER SIX

HOW CAN WE DIAGNOSE PCOS?

How can we diagnose PCOS?

Symptoms that we discussed earlier are important to diagnose PCOD. Mainly delayed periods (more than 35 days or 6 months) are the major sign. Other signs for diagnosis are:

- Blood sample: High levels of androgen (male hormone)
- Ultrasound: PCOS can be verified through ultrasound
- Blood sugar level/hb1c, cholesterol and triglyceride levels - PCOD make people insulin resistant.
- There isn't a single test that can be used to identify PCOS because it is a condition in which different women might have a variety of indications and symptoms. Blood is drawn to measure androgen levels, sugar or insulin levels, and other hormones as part of the PCOS test (thyroid, prolactin, adrenal hormones). To determine whether a woman has PCOS, it is recommended that she gets the ultrasound done of her ovaries. During this examination, the number of tiny sacs filled with fluid known as "follicles" should be counted.

CHAPTER SEVEN

WHICH ORGANS ARE INCLUDED IN THE PCOS?

Which organs are included in the PCOS? The following are the organs included in PCOS:
- Ovary is the female genital organ present on both sides of the uterus, it produces the female egg or ovum.
- Adrenal gland which is placed just above the Kidneys.
- Pancreas gland that produces insulin in our body.
- Pituitary gland, the gland below the brain which is responsible for all the hormonal control, especially for PCOS.
- The uterus where the main event for PCOS happens.

CHAPTER EIGHT

WHEN CAN PCOS HAPPEN IN THE BODY?

When can PCOS happen in the body ?

PCOS generally happens after puberty around 10 years to the menopause age of 45 - 50 years. Especially it shows itself around the fertility period (23-38 years approx) in women. It happens mostly on obese females, as the metabolic rate becomes slow which makes the body's hormonal system less active and more toxic for the endocrine system, starting with the pituitary gland. So it is mainly because of extra male hormones developing in the body which disturbs the synchronization of the body's hormonal system.

CHAPTER NINE

HOW PCOS AFFECTS THE BODY IN THE LONG RUN ?:

How PCOS affects the body in the long run ?:

PCOS symptoms can have a grave impact on one's confidence and self-esteem. These symptoms can also cause mental health issues like melancholy, anxiety, and mood swings. According to one such study, women with PCOS may experience much more psychological anguish than the women without. There are also some side-effects of PCOS like diabetes, cardiac complications like hypertension or low BP for cholesterol problems breast cancer and depression, and in the worst cases, also cancer. Others are high cholesterol, and infertility, however, we can cure it with yoga and lifestyle changes that we will discuss in further questions.

CHAPTER TEN

Is it possible to get pregnant with PCOS ?

Is it possible to get pregnant with PCOS ?

One can get pregnant despite having PCOS. The person needs to maintain a healthy weight, control glucose levels, and treat associated PCOS symptoms with changes in the lifestyle and medications. Also, it is advisable To keep track of the time of your period, using an ovulation calendar or an app. This allows you to make a better judgment of fertile days for better results. Your blood sugar levels are also important for getting pregnant and having a healthy pregnancy and ensuring the foetus's health. in many cases, some kitchen herbs, physical activities, Yoga, and naturopathy can assist you in getting pregnant.

CHAPTER ELEVEN

WHY IT IS IMPORTANT TO MANAGE WEIGHT & GLUCOSE LEVELS IN PCOS?

Why it is important to manage weight & glucose levels in PCOS ?

When the fat tissues and sugar levels are high, the woman suffers heavy weight and the ovaries are stimulated to create additional hormones like testosterone and other factors for developing insulin resistance. Issues like unwanted hair growth, irregular menstruation periods, and weight gain are the result of this. PCOS is exacerbated by insulin levels as well. So PCOS symptoms are interconnected with obesity and body sugar levels in the body.

CHAPTER TWELVE

WHAT TYPE OF FOOD CAN WE HAVE IN PCOS?

What type of food can we have in PCOS?

"Food is our medicine and the main medicine is our food. "

The main thing in one's lifestyle is food which is expected to be healthy food. As per the ayurveda food concept, PCOS is because of Kapha and Vata misbalancing in the body, so in order to balance them, healthy food is essential. Because, as we all know healthy food is like the more colours on one's plate with fruits and vegetables which are near to nature.

As part of this book, we have also provided the following which can refer at a later section of this book:

- Recommended food pattern for PCOS.
- The food list of PCOS and healthy food replacements.

CHAPTER THIRTEEN

WHAT KIND OF FOOD CAN WE TAKE MORE OR LESS IN OUR DIET?

What kind of food can we take more or less in our diet?

Here, we have shared a list of foods one can take in adequate quantities for PCOS, and also some foods which are to be taken in limited portions. Some foods to avoid have also been listed, along with their healthy substitutes.

- Packed Juice to be replaced by- Fresh Lime Juice, Fruits, Butter Milk, and Coconut Water.
- White Sugar is to be replaced by -Natural Honey, Jiggery, Mishri, Desi Bura, Khand .
- White Salt is to be replaced by - Rock (sendha) Salt, Black salt(max 5gram).
- Refined Oil is to be replaced by - Cow's Ghee, Filtered Oil.
- Namkeen is to be replaced by - Murmura, Roasted Makhana, Roasted Cereals, Chana.
- Frozen food is to be replaced by - Fresh food & Salad/Juice.
- Ready-to-Cook Food is to be replaced by: Fresh cook food and Seasonal Fruits & Vegetables.

CHAPTER FOURTEEN

Is fasting helpful in PCOS?

Is fasting helpful in PCOS?

Yes, fasting is an effective method to eliminate the toxins from the body and mind, and is best for balancing the tridoshas which are Vata, Kapha, and pitta but with an expert's supervision. There are many types of fasting such as mono-diet, water fasting, 2-day fast, fruit fast, vegetable salad fast, lemon water, juice fast and also intermittent fasting which is very convenient and is easy to follow. Hence, fasting will surely help cure PCOS along with Lifestyle changes, Yoga & Wellness methods . You can follow the fasting protocol for PCOS mentioning in the diet pattern

CHAPTER FIFTEEN

WHAT ARE THE NATURAL WAYS AND NATURAL EASY HOME REMEDIES FOR PCOS?

What are the natural ways and natural easy home remedies for PCOS?

Here are 8 most easy home remedies for PCOS-

1. Amla and turmeric powder, taken ½ tsp each, for an empty stomach is effective to decrese Kapha and Vata dosha.

2. Drinking triphala tea. For this, Take triphala powder with a pinch of salt (¼ tsp Triphala and 1 cup of water boil with a pinch of salt) and have it at bedtime, and it will prove to be very effective for eliminating the toxins from one's body.

3. Taking lemon water with jaggery as the first meal of the day gives good results in PCOS.

4. Shatwari is a good female tonic to balance the female hormone and give good results in PCOD/PCOS.

5. Having buttermilk with rock salt and jeera, black pepper, and pipli also gives good results.

6. Handful of cashew nuts in the evening snack is the best for irregular and scanty periods.

7. Regular sunlight (morning) or sunrise, gazing with closed eyes also improves vitamin D levels in the body, also having sun-charged water daily is an easy way for regulating vitamin d levels.

8. Nature walk, trekking or nature trail once a week in the lap of nature, makes your body auto tune with the five elements to get good results in PCOS.

CHAPTER SIXTEEN

WHAT CHANGES IN THE LIFESTYLE ARE BEST FOR PCOD/PCOS?

What changes in the Lifestyle are best for PCOD/PCOS?

The following changes are advisable for treating PCOD-

- 1. Trying to make the sleep cycles regular, by fixing a proper time for rise and for sleep.
- 2. Trying to follow the diet pattern (that we have shared in the diet module)
- 3. Regular yoga and pranayam practices under expert supervision .
- 4. Trying to make yourself feel near to nature, and to get enough time with mother nature.
- 5. Trying to use those 8 effective easy home remedies (last question) for the same.
- 6. Try to be physically and mentally active, and follow your passion, interests and hobbies.

CHAPTER SEVENTEEN

How does the Ayurveda concept help in PCOS?

How Ayurveda concept helps In PCOS?

Ayurveda identifies PCOS as a Kapha and Vata condition which causes an imbalance in the functioning of ovulation. After affecting the digestive fire - Jatharaagni - Kapha begins to disrupt the metabolic aspect of the seven tissues called Dhatu Agni. Each Dhatu Agni is responsible for the nutrition and production of the tissue in which it lives. In the case of PCOS, the dhatus involved are rasa dhatu (lymph and plasma), meda dhatu (adipose tissue), and artava dhatu (the female reproductive system). Ama, upon entering the cells of arthavadhathu, begins to impact the cellular intelligence of the cell by dampening pitharaagni, producing errors in cellular function and intelligence. The failure of cellular intelligence is also manifested in the inhibition of apoptosis. After understanding the root causes of this disease, we can incorporate better remedies for the same.

CHAPTER EIGHTEEN

How does modern and ancient science help in PCOS?

How does modern and ancient science help in PCOS?
    The expanding significance of yoga and meditation in the treatment of several lifestyle conditions, including diabetes and PCOS, has also begun to be acknowledged by modern sciences. In addition to providing medication for the treatment of PCOS, doctors now advise their patients to practice pranayama and meditate for a regular period of time. Although the precise etiology of PCOS is unknown, we do have therapeutic choices. You have the option to do something about it with yoga and a natural, holistic way of life. However, to receive the benefits of your practice, you must be consistent. And the best part is that the quantity of advantages you enjoy is exactly proportional to how hard you work at your yoga practice. So even if you start very slowly and in a lighter mood, it will surely pay off! All you need to do is stop worrying about your life, and start living.

CHAPTER NINETEEN

HOW YOGA WORKS ON PCOS/PCOD?

How yoga works on PCOS/PCOD?

Yoga: Yoga science operates on far subtler and deeper levels than simply the physical and mental body. Yoga aids the release of deeply buried stress in the body, and mind which can help reduce PCOS symptoms. Asanas (yoga postures) for PCOS free up the pelvic area and encourage relaxation, while pranayama (breathing exercises) are excellent tools for calming the mind. Along with them, some relaxing meditations function on a deep level to detoxify and de-stress the total system. Yoga helps to balance the tridosha in the body. Here we are giving detailed yoga postures with the pictures of the author for better understanding. According to your time you can practice yoga regularly with the included Yoga Modules.

According to a recent study, practicing yoga may help reduce testosterone levels and relieve anxiety and melancholy symptoms in women with PCOS. Participants who attended a one-hour regular 5 days a week yoga class for three months lowered testosterone levels by 29%. In the study, 31 women with PCOS between the ages of 23- 42 were randomly allocated to either a mindful yoga group or a control group. Classes were held for one hour each for 5 days a week for three months. Endocrine, cardiometabolic, and psychological parameters were taken at the start of the study and again three months later. Researchers discovered that women who completed the yoga intervention (13 in total) had lower free testosterone levels (5.96 vs. 4.24).pg/mL; $P<0.05$). Free testosterone is a normal hormone that can be elevated above typical female ranges in women with PCOS. The Study participants also saw an improvement in measures of anxiety and depression. Yoga gives us a holistic approach with a perfect workout of body mind and Soul.

CHAPTER TWENTY

WHICH YOGA-ASANS ARE BEST DURING PCOS ?

Which Yoga Asanas are best during PCOS?

The following Yoga Asanas are best for PCOS-
1. Tadasana
2. Triyak tadasana
3. Nataraja asana
4. Surya namaskar
5. Butterfly pose (baddha konasana)
6. Chakki sanchalan
7. Bird pose
8. Camel Pose / supta vajrasana
9. Gomukhasana
10. Sarvangasana
11. Matsyasana
12. Pawanmuktasana
13. Merudandasana
14. Shavasana
15. Omkar chanting
16. Kapal bhati kriya
17. Anuloma viloma pranayama

18. Bharmeri pranayama
19. Ujjayi pranayama
20. Breathing awareness
21. Counting of thoughts.
22. Kunjal kriya
23. Jalneti.

Yoga asana methods with their respective pictures:

i. **Tadasana Standing pose:**

Tadasana

- • Stand erect on the mat, toes should be parallel with at least a 5-7 inch gap.
- • Stretch your hand up, heels up with inhale, exhale slowly come down.
- • Synchronize it with your breath. If you can hold the posture make you're breathing normally.
- • Feel the stretch on heels, ankle, thigh, lower abdomen, and hand.
- • Relax. Repeat it for 5-7 rounds.

2. Triyak tadasana:

Triyak Tadaasna

- Standing pose
- Stand in tadasana
- Grip your fingers crossed and stretch your hand left and right ..exhale down, inhale up, and hold for 30 secs to 1 min with normal breathing.
- Come back straight.

    Relax

3. Natrajasana:

Natraj asna

- Standing pose
- Hold the right leg with the right hand, behind the back and stretch the left-hand front side.

- Try to make balance on one leg, and concentrate on any stable point.
- Repeat it with the other side.
- Relax

4. Surya Namaskara:

Surya namaskar chart

1. Tadasana

2. Padahastasana (Forward Bending):
3. Ashwa sanchalan (with right leg)
4. Tolasana (balance pose)
5. Rabbit pose
6. Sashtang pranam
7. Bhujangasana
8. Mountain pose
9. Rabbit pose
10. Ashwa sanchalan
11. Padahastasana
12. Tadasana Relax.

1. Tadasana: Stand erect on the mat, toes should be parallel; at least 5-7 inch gap. Stretch your hand up, heels up with inhale, exhale slowly come down to forward bending.

2. Padahastasana (Forward Bending): After the tadasana starts with an exhale stretch, you hang the front side on the floor, knee straight.

3. Ashwa sanchalan (with right leg): Inhale, both hands on the mat parallel to left toe and stretch right leg back with toe support (as picture shown).

4. Tolasana (balance pose): Exhale both legs on the back side and back and neck straight.

5. Rabbit pose: Exhale, place your knee on the mat, sit on the heels, and head on the mat.

6. Sashtang pranam: Exhale, lie down on your chest, and lift your hip.

7. Bhujangasana: Inhale, lift your head and chest up like a snake, knees slightly up from the mat.

8. Mountain pose : Exhale, head down hip up, heels on the mat like a mountain pose.

9. Rabbit pose : Exhale same as the 5 th pose.

10. Ashwa sanchalan : Inhale same as 3 rd pose.

11. Padahastasana: Exhale the same as 2 nd pose.

12. Tadasana: Inhale the same as the first pose. Relax .

5. Butterfly pose (baddha konasana):

Butterfly posture

- Posture: sit in dandasana, toes together and knees bend .
- Try to make them up and down like butterfly fluttering. With normal breathing.
- Try to touch the floor with both knees.
- After 1 minute, knees to come together and stretch legs straight and relax in dandasana.

6. Chakki sanchalan:

Chakki sanchalana

Sitting pose :
- Process: legs apart, make a grip with your fingers and rotate them click wise at least 20-24 rounds.
- Inhale, bend front and exhale back.
- Complete the round and legs together and relax.

7.Birdpose:

Bird Pose

- • Procedure: legs apart in sitting pose, inhale and stretch your both hands up, exhale, try to hold your toes with hands like you are, fly like a bird, spread your wings.
- Hold for some time with normal breathing.
- Slowly inhale and come back in dandasana.

8. Camel Pose / Ustra asna:

Camel pose

- Process: sit in vajrasana, stand on the knees and hold your back or heels (as per your capacity), drop your neck down and hold the posture with normal breathing.
- Slowly exhale, come back in vajrasana and relax.

9.Gomukhasan:

Gomukha asna

- Process: Sit in dandasana, fold your right leg, place your right toes beside the left hip, and fold your left leg the other side like cross your knee

- With hand hold the fingers on back side of neck but the same hand up as the leg.
- Hold it for some time with normal breathing.
- Relax and do it with the other side too.

10. Sarvangasana:

Sarvangasana (shoulder stand)

- Process: Supine pose
- Lift both legs at 30, 60 ,90 and 130 degrees, hold your back, make it straight like 90 degrees from the neck side.
- With normal breathing hold the posture and slowly come back with a 130, 90, 60 and 30 degree angle like the picture. Relax

11. Matsyasana :

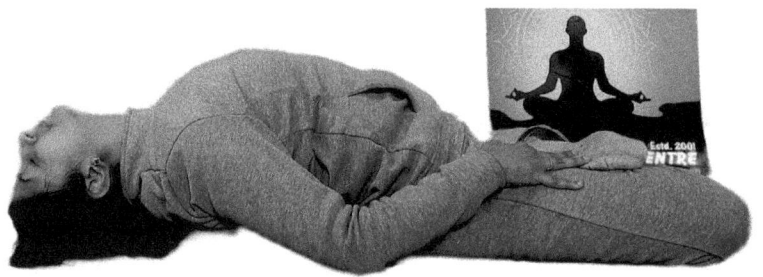

Matasya asna (Fish pose)

Supine pose:
- Do the padmasana and lie down on the back, lift your shoulder up and place your top of the head on the mat
- place your palm the thigh or hold the toe. Hold it with normal breathing.. and relax.

12. Pawanmuktasana :

Pawanmuktasana

supine pose:
- Bend your both knees and place them on the chest and make a grip with your fingers crossed to press the knees on the chest
- Hold it with normal breathing. And relax.

13. Merudandasana:

Merudanda asna

supine pose : • Lie down on the back, bend your knee and place your both knees at one side and neck on the other side to twist your spinal cord.

• It's a good and soothing stretch for the spine and supporting organs .

• Do it with your side too.

14. Shavasana:

Shavaasna

supine pose :
- After the yoga practice relax your body like you have surrendered to the mother earth
- Legs apart, palm facing the roof and just relax ...
- Some deep breaths and observe the body in the best relaxing pose. and awareness of each organ to make them more relaxed.

15. Omkar chanting:
Sitting or lie down pose: Like a you are surrender to the mother earth, melting on the mat.
- First start with inhale and chant aum 3 times to release the stress and stiffness from the body.

Aum...... Aum...aum...

16. Kapal bhati kriya:
Sitting pose :
- Sit in a comfortable pose, spine erect and start with an active exhale and continue for a min
- Afterwards just watch your breath (slowness and steadiness) .
- Try to make it like an active exhale with a relaxed and smiling face. But please don't move your abdominal area during the practice..it's a natural reaction during an active exhale so don't do it with any effort.
- After a min break ,one can make the next round for better results.

17. Anuloma viloma pranayama:

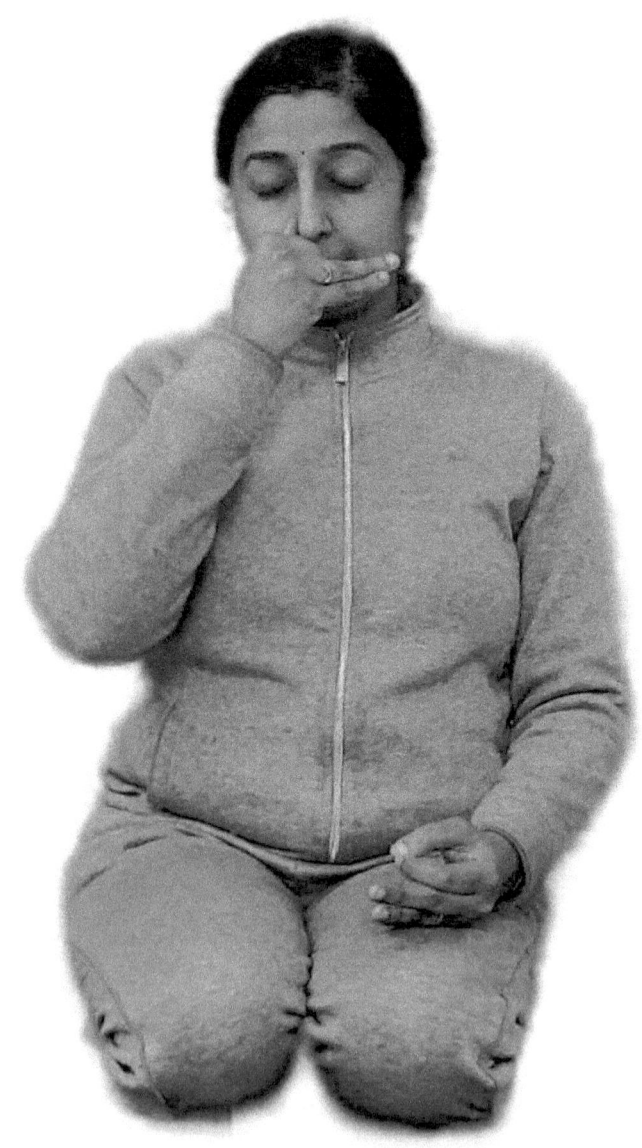

Anuloma viloma Pranayam

Sitting pose:
- Make nasika mudra like in the picture, sit comfortably and straight.
- Start the exhale from left and inhale, afterwards repeat it from right nostril exhale and inhale , continue to repeat it like this only.
- Make your breath more deep and effective like, exhale is longer than inhale.
- Do some rounds as your capacity or module and relax and enjoy the silence, balance in the body, mind and soul.

18. Bharmeri pranayama:

Bharmeri

Sitting pose:
- Sit in any meditative pose, close your ears and eyes and chant mmm..Kara like honeybee sound with lips together and do it 5-7 rounds or as per your modules.

- Relax and feel the change and resonance in the mind.

19. Ujjayi pranayama : .

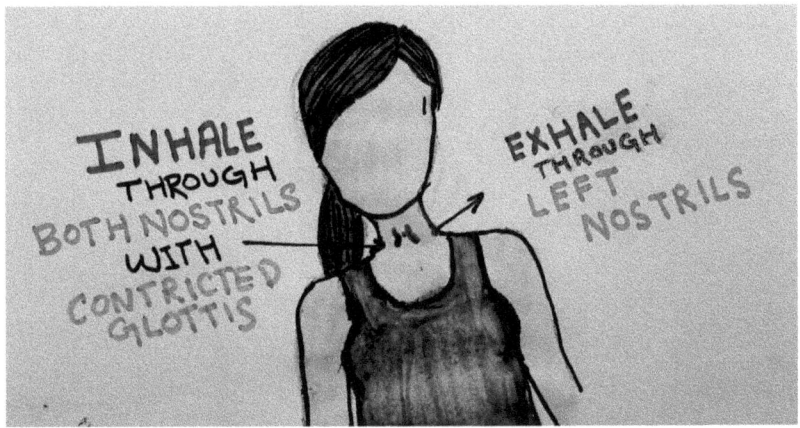

Ujjayi

Sitting pose:
- Inhale like seashore sound with the throat and exhale through the left nostril.
- It's a relaxing and refreshing practice for hormonal balance and stress management.

20 . Breathing awareness :

meditative pose

Sitting pose: • After all these pranayama practice do the anapana kriya to follow your breath, watch your breath, whichever nostril is active and let it be natural, as to make yourself more calm and relaxed and focused. • Do it according to your convenient modules.

21. Counting of thoughts:

Meditative pose :

- Just sit and count your thoughts as you are counting 123 .. don't try to chase them or any imagination..
- Sometimes one feels more thoughts or sometimes you are waiting for the thought to count...
- When you feel the waiting for thoughts, just enjoy the beautiful silence and balance of the mind..this is called an easy and practical technique for meditation. continue as per your modules suggests.

22. Kunjal kriya : (shatkarma)

KUNJal Kriya

Things you need: 1.5 to 2 liter lukewarm water, ½ TSP rock salt, 1 glass

Process:

- Sit in crow pose, drink this lukewarm salted water till you feel like vomiting,
- Stand on both feet together, left hand on navel, rub your tongue with right hand two fingers and automatically water comes out from stomach..till you feel empty from stomach.
- Do it with closed eyes and feet together. Do savasana after the practice of kunjal.

23. Jal neti:

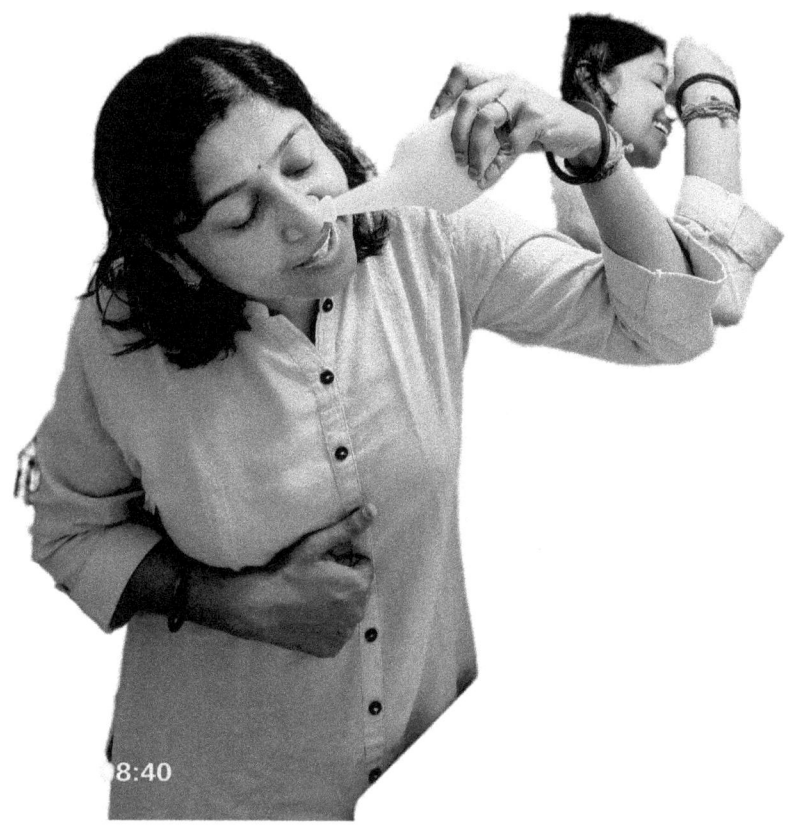

Jal neti

Things you need: 1 jal neti pot, 1 liter lukewarm salted water.

- Process: Fill the saline water in the netipot, Insert jalneti nozzle into the nose and twist your head to support the gravitation meanwhile do mouth breathing, automatically water comes out from the other nostril ..
- Make your comfortable with the posture, do it in a relaxing way..

- Repeat it with another nostril. After the practice do the kapalbhati kriya and bhramari pranayama to release the extra water from the sinuses.

CHAPTER TWENTY-ONE

How can we do yoga in less than 15 mins for PCOD/PCOS?

21. How can we do yoga in less than 15 mins for PCOD/PCOS?

Yoga is very effective for PCOD/PCOS, if you have less time like 15-20mins, here we have provided the module of for effective practice. Try to do some breathing practices too to get better results.

Yoga module:

15 mins schedule:

Posture	Rounds	Time
Surya namaskar	5-7 rounds	8 mins
Kapalbhati kriya	2-3 rounds	3 mins
Savasana		2 mins
Omkar chanting	3 rounds	2 mins

15 mins schedule

CHAPTER TWENTY-TWO

HOW CAN WE DO YOGA FOR 30 MINS FOR PCOD/PCOS?

22. How can we do yoga for 30 mins for PCOD/PCOS?

It's good if you want to give time for yoga, as the best results are in the regular practice of 30-35 mins mins including breathing, stretching, and meditation practices followed by Shavasana. Here we have also included the module :

Yoga module:

-30 mins schedule

Posture:

Posture	Rounds	Time
Surya namaskar	5 rounds	6 mins
Tadasana	2- 3	2 mins
Baddha konasana (butterfly pose)	20 rounds	1min
Chakki sanchalan	25 rounds	1 mins
Bird pose	1 round	1 mins
Vakrasana	2 round (both sides)	2 mins
Sarvangasana	1 round	1 min
Matsyasan/ suptbaddhakonasan	1 round	2 mins
Pawanmuktasana	1 round	2 mins
Savasana with abdominal breathing	20 rounds	3 mins
Kapalbhati kriya	3 rounds	3 mins
Ujjayi pranayam	5 rounds	2 mins
Anuloma viloma pranayama	11 rounds	5 mins
Omkar chanting	3 rounds	2 mins

30 mins Schedule

CHAPTER TWENTY-THREE

How can we do yoga for 60 mins for pcod/pcos?

How can we do yoga for 60 mins for pcod/pcos?

It's good if you want to give time for yoga, as the best results are in the regular practice of 60 mins mins including breathing, stretching, and meditation practices followed by Shavasana. Here we have also included the module :

Yoga module:

45 - 60 mins schedule:

Posture	Rounds	Time
Starting prayer		2 mins with omkara chanting
Tadasana	2-3	2 mins
Triyak tadasana (side bending)	2 rounds	3 mins
Natraj asana	Both sides	3 mins
Surya namaskar	10-12 rounds	10 mins
Baddha konasana (butterfly pose)	20 rounds	1min
Chakki sanchalan	25 rounds	1 mins
Bird pose	1 round	1 mins
Gomukhasana	2 round	2 mins
Sarvangasana	1 round	1 min
Matsyasan/ suptbaddhakonasan	1 round	2 mins
Pawanmuktasana	1 round	2 mins
Savasana with abdominal breathing	20 rounds	3 mins
Kapalbhati kriya	3 rounds	3 mins
Ujjayi pranayam	5 rounds	2 mins
Anuloma viloma pranayama	11 rounds	5 mins
Omkar chanting	3 rounds	2 mins
Breathing awareness		5 mins
Counting of thoughts		5-7 mins
Relax and enjoy the changes		

45-60 mins module

ALL ABOUT PCOS

CHAPTER TWENTY-FOUR

HOW DOES NATUROPATHY WORK ON PCOD/PCOS?

How does naturopathy work on PCOD/PCOS?

Naturopathy: panch tatwa -**Akash, Prithvi, water, fire, air.**

Naturopathy defines disease within the form of toxins in the body, so mother nature heals by releasing toxins from the body. By following the below methods, we can make effective balance in the five elements of our body, to increase the healing energy of our body itself.

Akash: fasting, relaxation meditation(Savasana), nature walk.

Earth: Mud bath, mudpack on the lower abdomen, mud pooling.

Fire: Sunbathing with banana leaves, local steam on the abdominal area, and hot and cold packs for better blood circulation toward the uterus.

Air: Regular walking morning or evening, body massage, head massage, yoga asana, and breathing works (pranayama) with awareness.

Water: Epsom salt bath, steam bath, sitz bath, spinal cord bathing, jet spray on the spinal cord.

CHAPTER TWENTY-FIVE

DO'S AND DON'TS FOR PCOS?

Do's and don'ts for pcos ?

Here are some basic and effective recommendations:

1. Have a 2 tsp desi ghee in the food regularly on served food, not in the cooking. This is for a healthy gut and to balance the doshas and elements of our body.

2. Avoid milk and dairy products, as milk products are like an invitation to hormonal imbalance in the body. It also aggravates Kapha dosha in the body which is not good for PCOS.

3. You can have fresh homemade buttermilk, with some roasted cumin seeds and rock salt.

4. You can also have Aloevera and shatawari for regular periods and the good flow of your periods, and so you could improve your hemoglobin level in your body. 5. Avoiding white sugar and white salt in your diet to regularize your hormonal system, and to purify your body.

6. The best way of treating PCOS is to follow fasting therapy, once a week or once every 15 days. You can have a fast or a solo diet, mono diet with fruit and water, and lemon water with vegetable soup, to release all the toxins from the body.

CHAPTER TWENTY-SIX

DIET PATTERN:

Diet pattern:
Here is a specific PCOS diet pattern, easy to follow. We have also included one fasting day to detox the body, give rest to digestive system to re-energise.
Diet pattern:

ALL ABOUT PCOS

	Day 1	Day 2	Day 3	Day 4	Day 5	Day 6	Day 7	fasting day
Early Morning 6.30 AM	2-3 glasses of lukewarm water empty stomach and do sun bath.							
Morning 7:30 AM	Jeera Tea	Mulethi water	saunf water	jeera water	coconut water	jeera water	white petha juice	
7.30 am	1/4 tsp amla powder and 1/8 spoon of dry turmeric with this water							
9 am (Breakfast Options, you can choose any option for a day)	2 banana	1 plate vegetable upma	1 plate vegetable moong dal chilla	1 plate sprouts with cucumber, tomato, onion with some drops of lemon	any seasonal fruit you like the most	2 banana	boiled sprout chana salad with lots of seasonal vegetales.	1 glass lemon water
post breakfast	Soaked 1 Walnut, 8 Almonds and 10 Raisins,15 sunflower seeds and 1 tsp sesame seeds (have it with fruit breakfast)							
11:00:00 (Before Lunch)	cucumber, tomato, beetroot salad							
Lunch 1:00 - 2:00	Buttermilk (Roasted Cumin and black pepper) 2 makki Chapati with ghee + 1.5 Cup seasonal/ Green Veg. + Moong Dal	Fresh Buttermilk (Roasted Cumin and black pepper) 2 wheat bran (Jau) Chapati with ghee + 1.5 Cup beans / Green Veg.	Buttermilk (Roasted Cumin, kali mirch) 2 Wheat millet (Jwar) Chapati with ghee + 1.5 Cup Lauki / Green Veg.	Buttermilk (Roasted Cumin, salt ,kali mirch) 2 palak jau and wheatn Chapati with ghee + 1.5 Cup seasonal/ Green Veg. + Moong Dal	Buttermilk (Roasted Cumin) stuff palak chapati with mix vegetable subji	Buttermilk (Roasted Cumin) 2 multigrain Chapati with ghee + 1.5 Cup seasonal veg + bitter guard veg	Follow your Food cravings	vegetable raita with boiled corns
Post Lunch	Sit in Vajrasana and chew 1 tsp saunf							
05:00-05:30PM Evening Snack	roasted chana murmura with lemongrass tea/Brahmi tulsi tea + roasted makhana							seasonal fruits
Dinner 20:00-20:30PM	4 idly with coconut chutney	Vegetable Wheat daliya	Mix Veg Barley daliya	Sprout moong Dal + 2 chapatis with vegetables.	Mix Veg Khichri with 1 tsp desi ghee	2 chapati roll with lots of veggies stuffing.	Follow your Food cravings	2 dal chapatis with mix vegetable
After meal	1/2 tsp Fennel Seed , a 10 minutes slow walk							
At Bed time	triphala water (1 tsp triphala in a glass of lukewarm water with a pinch of water.)							
Water/day	(try to take 125 ml at a time with just sipping it slowly)	Follow your thirst at least 2-3 litres in a day.						

Diet pattern

DR. MONIKA BIJAKA AGRAWAL

CHAPTER TWENTY-SEVEN

Can you suggest a suitable food list for Pcos?

Can you suggest a suitable food list for Pcos?
Foods to be avoided:
- White sugar in any form
- Salt in any forms
- Tea and coffee (cold or hot both)
- All the plain white basmati rice
- Maida and Corn flour.
- All the dairy products as milk, curd, paneer, khoya.
- Avoid soya products like soybean, soya chap, soya badi etc.
- Avoid more processed and frozen products that has more chemicals in their processing.

Foods you can have:
- Green leafy vegetables
- Fresh seasonal fruits but not exotic
- Fresh seasonal locally grown vegetables like tomato, beetroot, all types of beans, broccoli, carrot, all types of gourds as bottle gourd, bitter gourd, round gourd, moringa leaves, beans.
- Seeds like kalonji, sesame, sunflower, flax seeds, chia seeds and pumpkin seeds.

- In nuts like almonds, walnuts, pistha, cashew nut, and coconut.
- Buttermilk fresh with jeera, mint and rock salt.

  foods to consume in moderation:
  - Honey, jaggary, mishri, dates for the options of sugar.
  - Cooking oils
  - Fruit juices , please prefer fruits.
  - Try to prefer boiled or roasted not oil or air fried foods.

CHAPTER TWENTY-EIGHT

DO YOU HAVE ANY SUCCESS STORIES ABOUT PCOS?

Do you have any Success stories about PCOS?

The following is one of the success stories of our fellow patient, Shirin (name changed on request) overcame PCOS, the natural way- How to treat P.C.O.S. naturally- An Inspiring Success Story:

Diagnosis of any disease is a very hard pill to swallow; especially if the person is young and ambitious. A commonly diagnosed disease at young ages is P.C.O.S. or Polycystic Ovary Syndrome. This situation can be worsened when P.C.O.S. is creating havoc in the person's personal, professional and social life and when the body is undergoing a million changes all at once. These problems- if accompanied by erratic and excruciating period pains, unpleasant acne, and weight gain can affect one's self-esteem, and that once lost can take years to regain. Thus, let us learn how 26-year-old Shirin overcame P.C.O.S. naturally through a balanced diet, holistic lifestyle, and regular Yoga practice, while also discovering the secret to living a healthy, worry-free life.

How to overcome PCOS- Shirin's Journey THE FIRST SIGNS OF TROUBLE- Shirin is a 26-year-old software engineer, who was hardworking, determined, and brilliant at her work until she got diagnosed with this disease. Shirin was continuously struggling with woes like office stress, relationship expectations and independently living in a cyber city while surviving on ready-to-cook food items, or fast food. To say that she was living the perfect life before the disease would be a lie; in fact, considering it to just be a mild, stressful lifestyle would also be an understatement, however, PCOS just added to her woes. The first sign that was evident to her was- Acne. She regularly suffered from flare-ups and sensitive skin. Continuously, she suffered from PMS symptoms like mood swings, irritation, anxiety, unusual cravings, and irregular periods. She began to feel more and more fatigued day-by-day and began to lose her interest in the work she once loved. She still had not realized that she had this disease before her colleagues advised her to visit a doctor and get it checked. So, after a few months of suffering, she finally decided to meet a gynaecologist. She got all sorts of checkups and tests done- like ultrasounds, blood sampling, and blood sugar levels. She went back the next day, only to be shocked to know that she suffers from a disease- P.C.O.S. The doctor advised her to start taking oral contraceptive pills and to begin hormonal therapy to regularize her periods. As the doctor noticed Shirin's shocked face, she assured her that it was not that serious and she did not have to worry. She affirmed that PCOS was rather common amongst women her age and that those 'pills' could sort it out. So, she believed the doctor and tried the pills. One month had passed by, however, she felt as though something was missing and that her improvement was just temporary. She knew that she had followed the doctor's orders correctly and had followed the medication properly, however, she didn't get the expected output. Now, poor Shirin was feeling guilty and had to undergo mild depression. She kept continuing her medications for a few more weeks until she came to a decision.

Let's see how Shirin plans to overcome PCOS.

A MAJOR TURN- DISCONTINUING MEDICATION AND RESORTING TO NATURAL TREATMENT.

After suffering for 2 whole months, Shirin decided to quit the medication she was given at present and research natural ways to cure her disease. As she started researching her problem, she found out so many new things she never knew. She also discovered that the medicines she was allotted were a major reason for lifestyle disturbances in one's body, and could aggravate gastrointestinal discomfort, causing bloating, migraine, and muscle aches. Shirin researched for about a week and prepared the following plan to treat PCOS naturally, with no side effects.

SHIRIN'S 6-STEP PLAN TO TREAT PCOS NATURALLY-

1. A proper diet plan and elimination of all artificial sugar- Shirin had started focusing on her diet, ever since she had been diagnosed with PCOS, however, she knew she was doing wrong, but what was she doing wrong? She was ignoring the fact that sugar and ready cook foods are a bad idea for people with low resistance, like pcos patients. So, she began taking a diet that comprised fruits, vegetables, whole grains, legumes, and a side of proteins. Shirin had also eliminated all sorts of sugars, however, she had now begun using artificial sweeteners, which were way worse. She stopped it at once and switched to healthier substitutes like honey and dates. It was amazing how desserts could taste even better with honey or dates rather than artificial sweeteners or sugar. It was also an easy way for your taste buds to accommodate to a way healthier sweetness in your life..

2. Regular Yoga/Exercise- The best way to improve your health in any health condition is exercise. However, Shirin's hectic lifestyle suggested otherwise. A walk in the fresh air can not only cure your health but help keep you mentally stable as well. It helped her beat fatigue and stress. Regular Yoga practice is also advised, as the natural ways of naturopathy can help cure any disease, either fatal or mild. Thus, regular Yoga practice, 5 times a week and for an hour daily is advised. It also helps in de-stressing and beating depression. 3. Adding healthy food to your diet -Adding healthy food can help in weight loss, acne, and insulin resistance, which are common during PCOS. Thus adding foods like curd, cottage cheese

and kombucha can help beat PCOS.

4. Understanding the magic of (Kitchen herbs) such as Aloe vera and shatwari -these are miracle plants, good for the skin, the gut health, and treat sensitive skin and dryness. These have anti-inflammatory, antiseptic, and astringent properties that can help treat the underlying causes naturally.

5. Drinking adequate water: Drinking water, in our view, is the easiest way to flush out all the toxins in one's body. Not only does it balance the pH balance in our body, but it also helps with bloating, common in PCOS. A major reason for bloating is water retention in our bodies. It is not only advised but is essential to drink at least 3-4 litters of water per day to stay hydrated.

THE OUTPUT- Freedom from PCOD

Within 2 months of introducing these new changes, Shirin's body began to change, in a very good way. Following a properly balanced diet, going for a jog daily, joining our Yoga classes, understanding the magic of kitchen herbs, and drinking adequate water changed her life. Earlier, her period used to come whenever, but now it has been coming, in 28-29 days, regularly. Shirin has started noticing changes in her skin as well, as it had become more moisturized and was now mostly acne-free. Now, her stomach was rarely bloated and she felt much better about her work now, better than she felt before PCOS. She now had learned to make time for herself and her body, and to give herself at least 2 hours a day for practicing Yoga or Going for a jog in the fresh air. Being diagnosed with PCOS changed Shirin's life for the better. Today, she lives a healthier, happier, and much more active lifestyle which is suitable for her and her body in all aspects. She now lives the healthiest version of herself, all thanks to the changes she introduced in her life, and proved, that PCOS can be cured the natural way.

Hence, we should all be inspired by Shirin's journey and quit the allopathic, non-organic path of treating PCOS...... She recommends our Yoga classes for curing PCOS naturally, and has given our yoga centre @yogahealthcarecentre the following feedback-

"Dr. Monika is an extremely professional and wonderful teacher, who helped me overcome a time of disease when I had been diagnosed with PCOS. Being in corporate, we people are always prone to problems like stress, back pain, and likewise issues. I joined her Yoga classes a while back, 2 months after getting diagnosed with PCOS. Every day I used to come, stressed, teary, and disappointed with my life and job. I was discontent at all times, however, As soon as I used to enter the class, I felt positive and better. Dr. Monika, our smiling yoga guru used to make the environment much better and made us feel much more positive. Every day, I used to become a whole different person after the class, than before the class and the reason was- Dr. Monika. I truly believe that no other teacher could have made me feel so much better and satisfied with my life, only Dr. Monika could. She used to advise me to relax and be calm and helped with my PCOD. Within 2 months of regular yoga practice and following other natural measures, I was once again a PCOS-free woman, better than before or ever. Thank you so much, Dr. Monika, you are a major reason that my PCOS parted ways with me and now I live a stress-free life. I always regretted that why I did not know her and her class before I had to suffer for 3 months of excruciating pain because of the allopathic ways that my doctor had advised me to follow to cure PCOD. Indeed, Dr. Monika, you did wonders for me by making me realize how to live without my mobile phone and glasses for an hour which I thought I could only leave while sleeping. You taught me a new way to live, I can't thank you enough Doctor. I hope you keep smiling your beautiful smile and keep helping many others learn the better side of life...."-Shirin

Praise For Our Works

"*It was delightful to take prenatal yoga classes with you Monika ji. I loved stopping my busy life and taking time to contimplate my baby, our health, the reverence and the feelings of gratefulness. The prenatal yoga helped me to be more peaceful and trust my body more! It helped to strengthen my previous uterus c-section scar and tone my pelvic muscles very much. Your positive energy boost me mentally and give physical strength.And your support during my 9th month has no words to say. Your service is impeccable. In this pregnancy I felt my real raw labour without epidural which I wished for. Atlast what I learnt is believe in the self, irrespective of the age and risk factors, can make wonders in our lives, that yoga and you has taught me.i would definitely recommend you to my near and dear.*
    Jasmine Rebah"

"*Yoga Health Care Centre is the best place for yoga in Gurgaon. After wonderful experience in normal yoga class , I joined Pregnancy yoga class and I must say that my 9 months of pregnancy were so smooth. After hectic office schedule, I enjoyed the classes in evening to release stress of full day and to give some me time to myself and my baby.Specially to mention Dr. Monika is very supportive and flexible with the timings and gives you a friendly atmosphere to talk, share and discuss your issues/concerns freely.*"
    Parul Sapra"

""*Excellent Yoga sessions! Great trainer- Monika ji..she is very positive and gives proper attention to each individual in both offline/ online class.*
    Recommended to everyone".

Payal Yadav"

"My perception of Yoga changed with Dr. Monikaji's meticulous approach. I, now, fully embraced this ancient practice and feel so refreshed after every class. Yes, it also makes my body flexible and i love to continue improvising with her guidance". –
Ramsai Surya"

"It's been two months since I joined for Yoga sessions with Dr. Monika ma'am and I can already see positive changes within body as well as calmness of mind. Throughout the sessions she's very motivating, energetic, and also at times uses humour to lighten the mood of the session. In addition to being an excellent yoga teacher, she has good knowledge of household cures, solutions to common health problems, and is a very helpful soul."
SAthya Umesh"

"I just wish if words would have been suffice to let you how blessed I feel to come across such a wonderful person like you. More love to you for making my life beautiful with your immense guidance. The sessions are always awesome. Thank you !!
Sapna Gupta"

"Going to this amazing Yoga class is the only time of the day when i can connect and interact with my inner self. I feel much more refreshed, energized and the environment is so calm and peaceful. All credits to our teacher Monika m'am who not only monitors our asanas but equally radiates positive vibes to all!
Sohini"

"Monika ma'am is the best yoga teacher; I was an active member in yoga classes since last year but due to location change have to move east Delhi. Since than I was trying to find a good yoga class but believe me I am not able to find ,it is not like that we don't have yoga awareness about it but it has a great impact how your teacher deals with you. I am finding lot of changes in my lifestyle and health and wanted to go back to those golden days when I am associated with Monika ma'am' yoga classes .thank you so much ma'am for your valuable guidance n moral support ..i am lack of words saying thanks to you.
   Neha Garg"

For Quick Refrences

Diet Pattern:

FOR QUICK REFRENCES

	Day 1	Day 2	Day 3	Day 4	Day 5	Day 6	Day 7	fasting day
Early Morning 6.30 AM	2-3 glasses of lukewarm water empty stomach and do sun bath.							
Morning 7:30 AM	Jeera Tea	Mulethi water	saunf water	jeera water	coconut water	jeera water	white petha juice	
7.30 am	1/4 tsp amla powder and 1/8 spoon of dry turmeric with this water							
9 am (Breakfast Options, you can choose any option for a day)	2 banana	1 plate vegetable upma	1 plate vegetable moong dal chilla	1 plate sprouts with cucumber, tomato, onion with some drops of lemon	any seasonal fruit you like the most	2 banana	boiled sprout chana salad with lots of seasonal vegetales.	1 glass lemon water
post breakfast	Soaked 1 Walnut, 8 Almonds and 10 Raisins, 15 sunflower seeds and 1 tsp sesame seeds (have it with fruit breakfast)							
11:00:00 (Before Lunch)	cucumber, tomato, beetroot salad							
Lunch 1:00 - 2:00	Buttermilk (Roasted Cumin and black pepper) 2 makki Chapati with ghee + 1.5 Cup seasonal/ Green Veg. + Moong Dal	Fresh Buttermilk (Roasted Cumin and black pepper) 2 wheat bran (Jau) Chapati with ghee + 1.5 Cup beans / Green Veg.	Buttermilk (Roasted Cumin, kali mirch) 2 Wheat millet (Jwar) Chapati with ghee + 1.5 Cup Lauki / Green Veg.	Buttermilk (Roasted Cumin, salt, kali mirch) 2 palak jau and wheatn Chapati with ghee + 1.5 Cup seasonal/ Green Veg. + Moong Dal	Buttermilk (Roasted Cumin) stuff palak chapati with mix vegetable subji	Buttermilk (Roasted Cumin) 2 multigrain Chapati with ghee + 1.5 Cup seasonal veg + bitter guard veg	Follow your Food cravings	vegetable raita with boiled corns
Post Lunch	Sit in Vajrasana and chew 1 tsp saunf							
05:00-05:30PM Evening Snack	roasted chana murmura with lemongrass tea/Brahmi tulsi tea + roasted makhana							seasonal fruits
Dinner 20:00-20:30PM	4 idly with coconut chutney	Vegetable Wheat daliya	Mix Veg Barley daliya	Sprout moong Dal + 2 chapatis with vegetables.	Mix Veg Khichri with 1 tsp desi ghee	2 chapati roll with lots of veggies stuffing.	Follow your Food cravings	2 dal chapatis with mix vegetable
After meal	1/2 tsp Fennel Seed, a 10 minutes slow walk							
At Bed time	triphala water (1 tsp triphala in a glass of lukewarm water with a pinch of water.)							
Water/day	(try to take 125 ml at a time with just sipping it slowly)	Follow your thirst at least 2-3 litres in a day.						

Diet Pattern

15 mins Module for yoga for PCOS

Posture	Rounds	Time
Surya namaskar	5-7 rounds	8 mins
Kapalbhati kriya	2-3 rounds	3 mins
Savasana		2 mins
Omkar chanting	3 rounds	2 mins

15 mins yoga module

-30 mins Module for Yoga for PCOS

Posture	Rounds	Time
Surya namaskar	5 rounds	6 mins
Tadasana	2- 3	2 mins
Baddha konasana (butterfly pose)	20 rounds	1min
Chakki sanchalan	25 rounds	1 mins
Bird pose	1 round	1 mins
Vakrasana	2 round (both sides)	2 mins
Sarvangasana	1 round	1 min
Matsyasan/ suptbaddhakonasan	1 round	2 mins
Pawanmuktasana	1 round	2 mins
Savasana with abdominal breathing	20 rounds	3 mins
Kapalbhati kriya	3 rounds	3 mins
Ujjayi pranayam	5 rounds	2 mins
Anuloma viloma pranayama	11 rounds	5 mins
Omkar chanting	3 rounds	2 mins

30 mins yoga module

FOR QUICK REFRENCES

45- 60 mins Module for yoga for PCOS

FOR QUICK REFRENCES

Posture	Rounds	Time
Starting prayer		2 mins with omkara chanting
Tadasana	2- 3	2 mins
Triyak tadasana (side bending)	2 rounds	3 mins
Natraj asana	Both sides	3 mins
Surya namaskar	10- 12 rounds	10 mins
Baddha konasana (butterfly pose)	20 rounds	1min
Chakki sanchalan	25 rounds	1 mins
Bird pose	1 round	1 mins
Gomukhasana	2 round	2 mins
Sarvangasana	1 round	1 min
Matsyasan/ suptbaddhakonasan	1 round	2 mins
Pawanmuktasana	1 round	2 mins
Savasana with abdominal breathing	20 rounds	3 mins
Kapalbhati kriya	3 rounds	3 mins
Ujjayi pranayam	5 rounds	2 mins
Anuloma viloma pranayama	11 rounds	5 mins
Omkar chanting	3 rounds	2 mins
Breathing awareness		5 mins
Counting of thoughts		5-7 mins
Relax and enjoy the changes		

45-60 mins yoga module

FOR QUICK REFRENCES

Some Pictures About Yoga Health Care Centre

PCOD Awareness workshop in Gurgaon police academy awarded by ACP Gurgaon

The corporate stress management session

Media presence

SOME PICTURES ABOUT YOGA HEALTH CARE CENTRE

Pictures about Yoga healthcare centre

Regular Yoga session

Pregnancy yoga session

Meditation session

Pictures about yoga health care centre

SOME PICTURES ABOUT YOGA HEALTH CARE CENTRE

Social Media Presence

Website: www.yogahealthcarecentre.com
    Instagram: https://www.instagram.com/yogahealthcarecentre
    Facebook: https://www.facebook.com/Yogahealthcarecentre
    Youtube: https://www.youtube.com/@YogaHealthCareCentre
    Profile on **Trust pilot with all the reviews**
    https://www.trustpilot.com/review/yogahealthcarecentre.com

Milton Keynes UK
Ingram Content Group UK Ltd.
UKHW020946280923
429557UK00014B/550